Emily Sheehan is an award winning playwright and theatre maker. Her play *Hell's Canyon* won the Rodney Seaborn Playwrights Award, was shortlisted for the Patrick White Playwrights Award, and was showcased play in Playwriting Australia's National Play Festival. In 2018 *Hell's Canyon* was presented at the Old 505 Theatre in Sydney and La Mama Theatre in Melbourne. *Hell's Canyon* is published by Currency Press. *Daisy Moon Was Born This Way* was commissioned by Q Theatre and performed at The Joan in 2017. Her play *Versions of Us* was commissioned by Canberra Youth Theatre and performed at the Ralph Wilson Theatre in 2017. In 2018 Emily directed *Faster,* a new work devised with a teenage cast, for Canberra Youth Theatre. Emily has worked as a script assessor and dramaturg for Playwriting Australia. In 2019 Emily is part of Melbourne Theatre Company's Women in Theatre program. She holds a Masters in Playwriting from the Victorian College of Arts (VCA).

Isabelle Ford (left) as Daisy and Ayeesha Ash as Parker in the Q Theatre production at the Joan Sutherland Performing Arts Centre, Penrith, in 2017. (Photo: Katy Green Loughrey)

Daisy moon was born this way

EMILY SHEEHAN

CURRENCY PRESS
The performing arts publisher

CURRENCY PLAYS

First published in 2019
by Currency Press Pty Ltd,
PO Box 2287, Strawberry Hills, NSW, 2012, Australia
enquiries@currency.com.au
www.currency.com.au

Typeset by Dean Nottle for Currency Press.
Cover image © Shelly Perry / Stocksy United.
Cover design by Julia Rich for Currency Press

A catalogue record for this book is available from the National Library of Australia

Contents

Currency Press acknowledges the Traditional Owners of the Country on which we live and work. We pay our respects to all Aboriginal and Torres Strait Islander Elders, past and present.

For my family,
Mum, Dad and Clare,
the biggest freaks, geeks and weirdoes I know.

INTRODUCTION

Emily Sheehan captures the voice of young people arguably better than any other Australian playwright. Her play, *Hell's Canyon*, knocked my socks off with its ability to capture the spikiness and vulnerability of young people growing into themselves and into the inhospitable landscape of adulthood.

Like that play, *Daisy Moon* beautifully expresses the place where childhood dances into adulthood, one foot forward, two steps back. The power of the child's imagination to create comfort, optimism, resilience and healing in the face of time's brutal introductions is powerfully evoked. So too is the simultaneous terror in and yearning for leaving childish ways.

Emily's characters can be crude, colloquial and petulant. And yet they are always softened by their unwillingness to jettison everything they spring from, despite their professed longing to escape. Their sense of alienation is defeated by their inability to switch off their private tenderness. They encapsulate the longing of youth to outgrow it, but there is always a subtle resistance or distrust in the need for adulthood's false certainties.

In both *Hell's Canyon* and *Daisy Moon*, is the unidentified character of Grief. In *Hell's Canyon*, it is explicit in the plot. In *Daisy Moon*, Emily has rendered it more opaque, like a cloud of feeling that washes over the characters in different ways, infusing them with suffering. As in the earlier play, they know that to graduate from childhood is to find—perhaps with difficulty—the strength to face life head-on.

Emily writes vibrant naturalistic dialogue that transports the reader or audience immediately into the world of the play. But she is also drawn to representing the inner worlds that sustain her characters and allow them respite from the 'real' world. This makes her places deft literary rendezvous between naturalism and fantasy which creates a profoundly affecting humanity.

It's a joy to read another play of Emily's which demonstrates that the inheritors of the Australian stage are respectful of the traditional text-based story-driven theatre that audiences want, but also utterly unique in using powerful theatrical devices that are emotionally authentic rather than sensational.

Daisy Moon is another beautiful work of Emily's, with her characteristic grasp of the subtleties of young people finding their way.

Emily gives younger audiences a chance to see their own metaphysical dramas realised vividly on stage. For older audiences, she reminds us of when the past and the future collided in a fragile but wondrous present that did not quite belong to either realm. This ability to engage the sensibilities of a wide audience is testament to her power, skill and humanity as a writer.

Joanna Murray-Smith
February 2019

Joanna Murray-Smith is a Melbourne playwrght, screenwriter and novelist.

Daisy Moon Was Born This Way was commissioned and first produced by Q Theatre and first performed in the Allan Mullins Studio at The Joan Sutherland Performing Arts Centre, Penrith, on 16 November 2017 with the following cast:

DAISY / GAGA	Isabelle Ford
NOAH	Andre Drysdale
PARKER	Ayeesha Ash
JIMMY	Mansoor Noor

Director, Nick Atkins
Dramaturg, Dom Mercer
Designer, Emma White
Lighting Designer, Benjamin Turner
Sound Designer, Donna Hewitt
Stage Manager, Karina McKenzie

CHARACTERS

DAISY, female, 14 years old
PARKER, female, 15 years old
NOAH, male, 17 years old, Daisy's brother
JIMMY, male, 17 years old
GAGA, female

LOCATION

Batemans Bay.

PUNCTUATION

/ indicates the exact point of interruption in overlapping dialogue.

… indicates the character is choosing not to speak and should be afforded this space.

NOTES

The playwright encourages collaboration with artists from diverse backgrounds in the realisation and presentation of this play.

This play can be performed without an interval.

THANKS

My love and thanks to Jane Bodie, Dom Mercer and Nick Atkins who all provided invaluable dramaturgy to the script.

ES

ACT ONE

The bus stop on Daisy Moon's front lawn. Except it's not a bus stop. It's the stage of a Lady Gaga concert.

In the darkness, fans cheer: 'We want Gaga! We want Gaga!'

Lights slowly rise on DAISY MOON. *Fourteen years old. Silver sequined UFO skirt, disco ball earrings. A crown of vintage troll dolls. And long-faded glow stick bangles.*

DAISY *is surrounded by a galaxy of gemstones made of homemade collages and glitter glue signs with swirling lyrics.*

GAGA: What's on your mind, Daisy Moon?

> GAGA *is a voiceover of Daisy's own voice, modulated and melodic.* GAGA *is like a super sassy Cheshire Cat.*

DAISY: Gaga, I'm thinking about changing my name. To Celeste. Celestial. Celestial Moon.

GAGA: That's tight. But then you wouldn't be Daisy anymore.

DAISY: Daisy's not so great.

GAGA: Transformation is in the air, girl. The energy at this precise moment in time is electrifying. So buckle up star-seed, and let the music guide you through new and exciting positions.

> GAGA *lets out a lengthy cough.*

Daisy, I can't make my show tonight. I have laryngitis.

DAISY: Is it a bacterial infection?

> GAGA *coughs again*

GAGA: Viral.

DAISY: The only cure is bed rest.

GAGA: Daisy, you're the only person I trust to take my place on stage tonight.

DAISY: You can count on me.

GAGA: Did you practise the song?

DAISY: Just like you told me.

> DAISY *puts on her sunglasses and picks up a sparkling ukulele. Nervous, she gulps.*

GAGA: Well?

DAISY: It's—it's scary! What if someone from school sees?

GAGA: Daisy, you don't wanna fit in. You wanna stand out. Way out. So far out they'll think you were from outta space.

> *An electric guitar chord buzzes in the air.* DAISY*'s glow stick bangles light up.*

> DAISY *sings an acoustic rendition of 'Born This Way' by Lady* GAGA.

SCENE TWO

The bus stop on Daisy Moon's front lawn.

DAISY: Four years ago today. Ten years old. Double digits.

Come into the kitchen and up at the bench, in my usual seat at the kitchen counter, Mum's bought Coco Pops and Milo. Yum! Chocolate for breakfast. Next to the cereal is a small, square present. Shimmery turquoise wrapping paper with an orange ribbon.

The card reads: 'Happy Birthday Daisy. Kiss kiss. Mum.'

I pull at the bow slowly. Peel back the sticky tape, and out slides a CD.

On the front is a pink neon triangle outlining a woman's face. She has super thick eyeliner and black lipstick. Ice-white hair swirling around her face.

In pink letters across the bottom of the CD reads: 'Lady Gaga Born This Way Two-Disc Deluxe Edition'.

And that was the beginning of the new me. Adult Daisy. See ya later, childhood. Hello, puberty.

I'm totally obsessed. I know the lyrics to every single song.
I beg Mum for a guitar but she buys me a ukulele.
'It's more portable,' she says.
'Yeah right. Rock stars don't play ukuleles.'
I learn all the chords.

Fast-forward, and Mum and I are on a Murrays Bus from Batemans Bay to Sydney Central Station. My first time in the city. We get off at Central and walk through Chinatown down to Darling Harbour, past the shops and traffic lights and footpaths packed with people, and massive concrete buildings, till we get to the Entertainment Centre.

Out on the promenade are so many people. Dressed up totally crazy. These freaks and geeks and weirdos. The misfits and the troublemakers. Little Monsters. That's what Gaga calls us. Her fans. We're her Little Monsters. The ones that don't fit in. The ones that stand out. Way out. So far out you'd think we were from outta space.

There's one group of girls in particular. Standing in front of a merch stand covered in all these awesome tees. I want one so bad.

'Please, Mum, please!'
'Forty bucks? Daisy, what about a key chain?'
'You said you didn't trust me with house keys.'
'Look, they have fridge magnets, they look nice.'
'No, I want a t-shirt! Please please please please please?'
'Forty bucks? There's just no way, Daisy.'

We get in line behind the group of girls. There's five of them.
All dressed like … like … like queens!
But not in tiaras and glass slippers.
In sequins and glitter and body paint.
Hairspray and eyeliner and stick-on diamantes.
Velvet and fishnets and tutus and hot-pink combat boots.

Teen. Weirdo. Royalty.

Head to toe their outfits say something. Their clothes scream: 'I'm different'. Their clothes scream: 'I don't care what you think'. Their clothes scream: 'Bow down to my creative genius or else!'

Queens like this don't care about palaces and princes.
Queens like this don't need no-one to save them.
Queens like this know how to save themselves.

The tallest, towering over the rest in platform sneakers, wet-look leggings, an aqua tutu, and a monster mask. She says to her friends, 'Lady Gaga is our church and music is our religion'.

And I get it.

I totally one hundred percent get it.

She must be one of Gaga's High Priestesses. Sent from the stars to planet Earth.

She buys a packet of glow stick bangles, so I turn to Mum and say, 'Don't worry about a t-shirt, Mum. I want those bangles.' They're so cool. Neon green and hot pink. Gaga's my church and music is my religion.

Then, inside the stadium, music starts blasting. Blasting so loud I can feel the bass notes in the concrete below my feet. The whole of Darling Harbour rumbles with Mother Monster's soundwaves.

'Mum, let's go in, it's starting!'
'Mum, I said it's starting!'
'Mummmm?!'

SCENE THREE

Noah's bedroom. Unlived in. No sheets on the mattress. Kmart bag in the corner. A cardboard box with the word 'TROPHIES' scrawled across it. On top of the boxes sits a portable radio which DAISY *uses for her dance rehearsal.*

DAISY *practises her choreography to 'Paparazzi' by Lady Gaga. She dances from the heart with expressive moves akin to performance art. It's surprisingly good.*

DAISY: Five, six, seven, eight!
'I'm your biggest fan,
I'll follow you until you—'
Three and four, five, six, seven, eight.
'Baby there's no other
Superstar you know that—'
Point and point, drop, jump!

NOAH *and* JIMMY *enter carrying cardboard boxes and a duffle bag.*

NOAH: That's my radio.
DAISY: Noah!

DAISY *bearhugs* NOAH. NOAH *doesn't hug her back.*

NOAH *dumps his duffle bag on the floor, examines his old room.*

NOAH: What's all this shit on the wall?

DAISY: The Batemans Bay Little Monsters Fan Club. This is now the number one safe space for the freaks and geeks of the South Coast.

JIMMY: She got the freaks and geeks part right.

DAISY: I heard that.

NOAH *opens his wardrobe, looks inside.*

NOAH: Get your crap outta here before dinner—

DAISY: Overruled! This space is booked daily from two p.m. There's a booking schedule on the door. Clubhouse meet-ups have been clearly outlined and colour-coded for your convenience.

NOAH: Oi, Daze, where's the box that was in my cupboard?

DAISY: I dunno.

NOAH: There was a cardboard box right there.

DAISY: I said I dunno, Noah.

NOAH: Where the fuck is it?

DAISY: You mean Dad's stuff?

Pause.

There was a box with Dad's jacket and some smokes.

NOAH: Where'd you put it?

DAISY: Nowhere. Mum musta chucked it.

JIMMY: Where is ya mum anyways?

NOAH: Probably still in bed.

JIMMY: Saw her down the shops last week.

Pause.

NOAH *and* DAISY *eyeball each other, unsure what to say to* JIMMY.

Nah, she actually looked alright.

DAISY: Why wouldn't she look alright?

An uncomfortable silence.

NOAH: Get out, Daisy, we're playing FIFA.

DAISY: Mum sold the PlayStation.

NOAH: Lucky for me, I own an Xbox now. Out.

DAISY: You get out of my clubhouse. This is a closed rehearsal.

NOAH: Daisy, this is my bedroom.

DAISY: Then, then … I'm playing Xbox with you.

JIMMY: I don't think this is your sort of game.

DAISY: That's gender stereotyping.

JIMMY: You wish you were a gender stereotype—

DAISY: That doesn't even make sense—

JIMMY: You don't even make sense—

DAISY: You don't even / know what sense—

NOAH: Daisy, shut it.

NOAH *sets up his Xbox during the following.*

DAISY: This room's been empty all year. I always use this room.

NOAH: Well, permission revoked.

DAISY: It's my birthday, by the way. In case you forgot.

NOAH: Happy birthday, loser. Out.

DAISY: Mum's doing cake after dinner.

NOAH: Since when does Mum cook dinner?

DAISY: I'm baking the cake but it was Mum's idea. She bought packet mix. And if you haven't got me a present yet—

NOAH: I haven't got you a present—

DAISY: Well, if you *haven't* got me a present *yet*, then what I'd *love* is three hundred bucks—

NOAH: I haven't got you a present—

DAISY: I know! I'm trying to *tell you* that what I would *love* is—

JIMMY: He's not doin' birthday cake, alright, he's busy.

DAISY: You're not invited, Jimmy, by the way.

JIMMY: Wouldn't show if I was.

DAISY: So I guess I'll see you later, Noah?

NOAH: Boys are doin' a bonfire tonight.

JIMMY: Unless ya busy with something else?

NOAH: Nothing jumps to mind.

DAISY: What about cake?

NOAH: Daze, fuck off already, how many times do I gotta tell you?

DAISY: If you're going to be *living here again*, Noah, then you have to actually try to be a decent person.

JIMMY: Live here again?

NOAH: I don't live here, it's just for summer.

DAISY: Liar.

NOAH: Daisy, leave it.

DAISY: He lives here now, Jimmy. Got expelled from boarding school.

NOAH: Shut up, Daisy.

DAISY: Perfect Noah got kicked out.

JIMMY: Since when?

DAISY: You'd know if you could read, Jimmy. It was all over the news-papers. Mum was humiliated. Shoulda heard her on the phone to Dad—

NOAH: Stop spewin' ya mouth off like ya know something 'bout it, when you actually know nothing, alright!

JIMMY: Mate, why didn't you say anything?

DAISY: He's clearly mortified he's not as good at swimming as we all thought.

NOAH: She's lying.

DAISY: Am not. His new school shirts are in that Kmart bag.

JIMMY: What the fuck, Noah, what about Nationals?

DAISY: Yeah, Noah, what about Nationals?

NOAH: [*approaching* DAISY] Listen, Daisy, this is how it's gonna be now. You don't come in my room, you don't touch my things, and you stay outta my face.

DAISY *doesn't back down, stares* NOAH *in the face.*

DAISY: Jimmy, guess why he's back? He got arrested and kicked off the swim team.

NOAH: Don't listen to her, Jimmy. She's a stupid little bed-wetter, who hasn't got her period yet. Now fuck off, you little freak.

DAISY*'s eyes well with tears, she bites her lip, tries her hardest to look tough.*

What? Are you gonna cry?

DAISY: I hate you. I really, really hate you.

DAISY *storms out.*

JIMMY: Is it true? You're starting back at Surfside Public?

NOAH: Dunno yet.

JIMMY: Well, when will you know?

NOAH: I don't wanna talk about it.

JIMMY: What happened?

NOAH: I said I don't wanna talk about it, Jimmy. Get it in ya head, alright?

JIMMY: I mean you coulda told your best friend.

NOAH: …

JIMMY: …

NOAH: You wanna be Manchester or the Spurs?

JIMMY: Spurs.

> NOAH *hands* JIMMY *the Xbox controller.*

You'll be one of us again.

NOAH: …

> NOAH *selects 'PLAY' with the Xbox controller.*

JIMMY: [*playing*] Have you played the new Resident Evil?

NOAH: Haven't had time.

JIMMY: They switched the live action to a first-person perspective so the infections and blood and stuff is like, very intense. Like, next level intense.

NOAH: Yeah?

JIMMY: It's a good switch. I prefer the deeper immersion of first-person shooter. I preordered online and then camped out to get it.

NOAH: I'm pretty over Xbox. I used to be really, really into it. Not anymore.

JIMMY: …

NOAH: You like Xbox though.

JIMMY: It's like my whole life.

> JIMMY *scores a goal.*

Howzatttttttt! Gotta keep your eyes on the screen, boy.

> *They play.*

> JIMMY *scores again.*

Ohhhhhhhhh!

> NOAH, *frustrated and distracted, stares into space.*

> JIMMY *presses buttons on the controller but nothing happens.*

You gotta hit play, Noah. Oi, Noah!

NOAH: Right. Sorry.

> NOAH *selects 'PLAY'.*

They play.

JIMMY *scores again.*

/ Dammit!

JIMMY: Goalllllll!

NOAH: Nah, I'm over it. Let's get outta here.

JIMMY: Ah-ah-ah, you can't quit coz you're down three goals. I don't
know how they do it in Sydney, but back home—

NOAH: It's FIFA. What are you, twelve?

JIMMY: We can go to mine and play Resident Evil?

NOAH: Course there's nothing better to do in this shithole town.

JIMMY: Wanna get high? Unless you're training tomorrow?

NOAH: I am. But that's tomorrow.

JIMMY: Sounds like future Noah's problem to me.

NOAH: Solid point.

JIMMY: Alright, my boy is back. Lemme text Lucas.

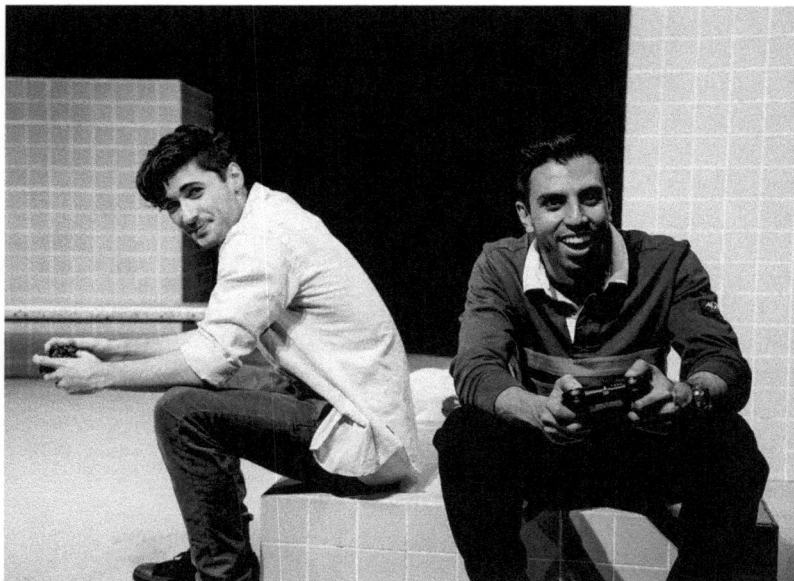

*Andre Drysdale (left) as Noah and Mansoor Noor as Jimmy in the
Q Theatre production at the Joan Sutherland Performing Arts
Centre, Penrith, in 2017. (Photo: Katy Green Loughrey)*

JIMMY *takes his phone out of his pocket. Begins a text message conversation with Lucas.*

NOAH: Wait up. Can you not mention to Lucas about the whole 'moving back here' thing? Actually, can you not mention that to anyone?

JIMMY: Course, mate. I'll take it to the grave.

JIMMY *'s phone buzzes.*

Lucas is sweet if you got cash?

NOAH: How much?

JIMMY: Fifty.

NOAH: Who's charging fifty?

JIMMY: Lucas.

NOAH: Why's Lucas charging us at all? The little worm easily owes me at least one hundred.

JIMMY: Well, he wants fifty. You want to or not?

NOAH: He has smoked like, hundreds of dollars of my pot. All of you have. You're always mooching off me. What an absolute insult that he would even suggest I pay him.

JIMMY: So it's a no?

NOAH: I'm not giving Lucas ten until he sucks my balls.

JIMMY: Fine, man, I'll give him fifty, and you can spend tonight eating a sorry-arse packet-mix birthday cake.

NOAH: We're not giving any money to Lucas. I got some pills anyways.

JIMMY: Pingers? In the middle of the day?

NOAH *takes a bottle of prescription medication from his duffle bag.*

NOAH: It's Ritalin.

JIMMY: You a mental now or somethin'?

NOAH *tosses* JIMMY *the bottle.* JIMMY *catches it and reads the label.*

Who's Alex?

NOAH: What?

JIMMY: Alex. His name's on the bottle.

NOAH: Boy in my dorm.

JIMMY: Is he the mental?

NOAH: You sound like a chav when ya talk like that.

JIMMY: You're gettin' defensive—
NOAH: I'm not defensive—
JIMMY: Is Alex your boyfriend or something?
NOAH: He's a lad in my dorm. And I nicked his meds, alright?
JIMMY: Why?
NOAH: You want 'em or not?

> JIMMY *opens the bottle and takes out a pill.*

JIMMY: Won't he notice 'em missing?
NOAH: All the boarders are swimming in cash, so ... he'll live.

> JIMMY *swallows the pill.*

JIMMY: [*handing the bottle to* NOAH] So you really back for good then?
NOAH: [*taking the bottle*] Reckon so.
JIMMY: One of us again.
NOAH: Same as before.

SCENE FOUR

The bus stop on Daisy Moon's front lawn.

DAISY *adamantly tapes up her clubhouse posters. She huffs and puffs in frustration.*

Glockenspiel musical scales and a UFO whir melodically in the air.
GAGA *is present.*

GAGA: What's on your mind, Daisy Moon?
DAISY: My psychic energy is all messed up.
GAGA: You're sending out some abnormal vibrations.
DAISY: Tell me about it.
GAGA: Take a seat in my office, moon-child. That's what I'm here for.

> DAISY *lies down on the bus stop bench as if it were a therapist's chair.*

DAISY: Gaga, can we talk about ... you know ... my noo-noo?
GAGA: Only if you never call it that again.
DAISY: Everyone has their period but me.
GAGA: You can't rush these things. You gotta let womanhood come to you.
DAISY: Please? It can be my birthday present.

GAGA: I'll see what Mother Monster can do.

DAISY: You know just what to say to a girl.

> *Pause.*

Gaga?

GAGA: Daisy?

DAISY: I'm special, right?

GAGA: Every creature Mother Monster puts on this planet is special.

DAISY: I'd rather be special than normal.

GAGA: Mmmm-hmmmm.

DAISY: I'd rather be dragon fruit than vanilla.

GAGA: Preach, sister.

DAISY: I'd rather be all alone in a clubhouse of one, than have to fit in with anyone else. I guess I'm just a lone wolf, Gaga. [*Howling*] Ah-woooooo!

GAGA: I used to be a lone wolf. Didn't work out. Wolves need a pack. Superstars need fans. And moons need a planet to orbit. Something to orbit gives a moon purpose. Otherwise you're just a big ol' hunk of space rock.

DAISY: I don't need a planet. I'm a lone moon. Catapulting solo through space.

GAGA: No such thing, girl. A moon ain't a moon without a planet.

DAISY: I don't need a planet.

GAGA: Sounds lonely to me.

> PARKER *enters. A magical chiming sound.*

PARKER: Are you Daisy?

DAISY: Who's asking?

PARKER: I'm here for the meeting.

DAISY: …

PARKER: The club meeting. The Batemans Bay Little Monsters Fan Club.

DAISY: How do you know about that?

PARKER: Saw the flyer.

> PARKER *takes a flyer from her pocket. It shimmers like the ocean.*

[*Reading from the flyer*] 'Greetings, Earthlings. Batemans Bay Little Monsters Fan Club is looking for new monsters. Meet at the Bus stop on Wakefield Street two p.m. every day this summer. RSVP by sending your psychic vibrations to Daisy Moon, Club President.'

DAISY: How'd you get that?

PARKER: So can I join?

DAISY: I have no idea what you're talking about.

PARKER: Well, do you want to hang out anyway?

DAISY: No thank you. I'm busy.

PARKER: Busy doing what?

DAISY: It's a secret.

PARKER: Busy doing clubhouse things?

DAISY: No, because there's no club.

PARKER: Then why are you wearing a badge that says 'Club President'?

DAISY: I'm being ironic.

PARKER: Then why are all those posters hanging up?

DAISY: I don't know. Maybe Banksy was here. He's been trying to get my attention, but I'm not interested.

PARKER: Look, if you don't want me in the club, you can just say so.

DAISY: There isn't any club for me to not want you in. I can't not want you in something that doesn't exist.

PARKER: Yeah yeah, I get it, there's no club. Wink, wink.

DAISY: Hey. Stop winking.

PARKER: Oh, is it a secret club? Because I can keep a secret.

DAISY: Just drop it, alright.

PARKER: Consider it dropped. [*Under her breath*] President.

DAISY: I heard that.

PARKER: Heard what? [*Under her breath*] President.

DAISY: I'm not the President.

PARKER: I know. [*Under her breath*] President.

DAISY: Seriously, stop that. I know you're bullying me, okay. Whoever put you up to this, ha-ha, very funny, joke's over. You can go tell Georgia and everyone else that it's completely embarrassing and no-one showed and I surrender.

PARKER: Who's Georgia?

   Silence.

   DAISY *avoids* PARKER*'s eye contact.*

I don't know who's messing with you, but I promise I'm not one of them. And for the record, you can't kick me out of a public bus stop. So I'm gonna stay.

PARKER *takes a seat next to* DAISY.

I'm Parker, by the way.

DAISY: What are you doing?

PARKER: Taking a seat.

DAISY: I kinda wanna be alone right now.

PARKER: Just waiting for a bus.

Long pause. The girls study one another.

DAISY: How long are you planning on sitting there?

PARKER *shrugs at her.*

Where you headed?

PARKER: Down the shops, I guess.

DAISY: Probably be faster for you if you walked.

PARKER: Doubt it.

DAISY: Public transport isn't really a 'thing' round here. You could walk faster to literally anywhere.

PARKER: Not to space.

DAISY: You could walk to NASA, train to be an astronaut, find a spaceship and fly to space faster than the buses show up.

PARKER: Wow, that sounds factual.

DAISY: Can't argue with science.

Pause.

PARKER: You know anything 'bout a New Year's Eve party? Heard some kids talking.

DAISY: Everything in this dumb town sucks. Including the parties.

PARKER: No way. There's a beach, and minigolf, and a pool, and a chicken shop, and … um … and this bus stop's kinda interesting.

DAISY: It's the worst. The beach is swarming with tourists, and some paedo owns the minigolf. Don't worry, he went to jail and his wife took over, but it gives the place a super depressing vibe. School's the worst. And no concerts ever happen here because there aren't enough people to fill a stadium.

PARKER: Like a Lady Gaga concert?

DAISY: Exactly.

PARKER: What's so bad about school?

DAISY: Nothing.

PARKER: Is that Georgia girl from your school?

DAISY: You ask a lot of questions.

PARKER: There's 'Georgias' at my school too.

DAISY: I don't get picked on. I have loads of friends actually.

PARKER: Will they get here soon?

DAISY: …

PARKER: You ever met anyone famous?

DAISY: Nup. But I will.

They sit in silence.

PARKER: Can I go with you to the party?

DAISY: Not going. Same night as the Lady Gaga concert in Sydney. I just need three hundred bucks for tickets and a bus pass.

PARKER: Cool.

DAISY: I'm gonna go wearing one of my creations. Then Gaga will see me in the crowd, and she'll just … just *know* that I'm the real deal. That Daisy Moon is a real life Little Monster! It's only my most deepest wish in the entire universe.

PARKER: What if you go and Gaga doesn't see you?

DAISY: She will.

PARKER: How do you know?

DAISY: I just know. You can't explain destiny. It's just a little humming underneath your skin that starts deep down in your bones.

PARKER: Like a bass note.

DAISY: Exactly.

> DAISY *surveys* PARKER. *Decides she likes what she sees.*

If you actually wanna join the club, I can make you a temporary member for twenty-four hours. As a trial.

PARKER: Yeah.

DAISY: Ten bucks.

PARKER: What?

DAISY: The joining fee is ten bucks.

PARKER: Are you messing?

DAISY: Hand on my heart, the membership fee is ten dollars.

PARKER: Alright.

> PARKER *takes a tenner out of her pocket.*

I guess now you only need two hundred and ninety bucks for concert tickets.

DAISY: How come I never seen you round here before?

PARKER: My parents are military. They're overseas waiting to hear about a posting in Berlin. Cool, hey? I'll be total Euro-trash.

DAISY: Nice.

PARKER: I'm staying at my grandparents' house for the summer.

DAISY: Which house?

PARKER: That blue weatherboard right across the street.

DAISY: Which one?

PARKER: That blue one there. Next door to the beaten-up shitbox. Yeesh, that place looks depressing.

DAISY: That's my house.

PARKER: Oh.

Awkward pause.

Sorry. I didn't know.

DAISY: Apology not accepted.

Silence.

PARKER: That's a … cool … necklace.

DAISY, *though tempted by the compliment, continues to ignore her.*

Where'd you buy it? At a Westfield?

DAISY: Eww no, I don't go to Westfield.

PARKER: I like Westfield.

DAISY: Well, I don't.

PARKER: You think you're better than Westfield? You're like *above* Westfield?

DAISY: I didn't get this at Westfield; it's a once-off, custom design. Because I made it. Custom. For myself. It's an homage to the meat dress Lady Gaga wore to the VMA Music Awards. The dress was made from raw meat. But this isn't raw. It's just my dinner from two nights ago. Take a look.

PARKER: I'm vegetarian.

DAISY: Were you born that way?

PARKER: Since I did a science assignment on the environment. Been going three weeks strong. I caved last week and at the pool and ate a sausage roll. But apart from that, I'm solid.

DAISY: Your secret's safe with me.

PARKER: My grandparents own the pool in town. They just opened a tuckshop. They need someone to work the till.

DAISY: Your grandparents own the pool?

PARKER: Yep.

DAISY: Your family owns an *actual* pool?

PARKER: Yep.

DAISY: Um, hello, you must literally have the best life ever!

PARKER: It's alright.

DAISY: It's a freaking *swimming pool*. You should be full-on milking that. You may as well be full-blown teen royalty.

PARKER: If you got any work experience I can tell 'em about you.

DAISY: I have hours and hours of experience. Stacking library shelves. At school. During detention.

PARKER: That's not work experience.

DAISY: It's child labour. Basically slavery.

PARKER: Slavery is actually way shittier than detention.

DAISY: Well, stacking library shelves, stacking tuckshop shelves. What's the diff?

PARKER: Why'd you get detention?

DAISY: Stupid rat-face Georgia was messing with me, and got these other girls involved, so then I—

Wait-wait-wait!

Is this my job interview? Or are you asking as a friend?

PARKER: So you want the job?

DAISY: What's the pay?

PARKER: Minimum wage.

DAISY: What's minimum wage?

PARKER: Six dollars seventy-three an hour.

DAISY: Nice.

PARKER: And guess what?

DAISY: What?

PARKER: Now we're work buddies!

DAISY: What?

PARKER: I work there too. So we'll be work buddies. We can catch the bus together, and hang out at the pool all day, and go swimming after our shift. I'll tell my grandma. Meet you back here seven a.m. tomorrow morning?

DAISY: Woah woah woah, this is all moving super fast.

A motor rumbles, the sound of the bus approaching.

PARKER: Hey, the bus showed. You wanna go to the beach? Gran says that's where all the kids meet up. Down by the chicken shop.

DAISY: Not me.

PARKER: Let's go down.

DAISY: I don't really go down there.

PARKER: You know a better spot?

DAISY: I gotta bake a cake tonight.

PARKER: It's two thirty.

DAISY: It's a super complicated recipe I've never attempted before.

    PARKER *looks at* DAISY *suspiciously, but decides not to push it.*

PARKER: Okay. Well, see ya seven a.m?

    DAISY *shrugs.*

    PARKER *exits.*

    DAISY *adjusts some of the* GAGA *paraphernalia on the bus stop walls.*

    NOAH *and* JIMMY *approach.*

DAISY: Get out of my clubhouse.

JIMMY: This is a literal bus stop, you psycho.

DAISY: Noah?

NOAH: [*mocking*] *Noah.*

DAISY: Can I have three hundred bucks?

NOAH: Absolutely not.

DAISY: I'll pay ya back.

NOAH: I don't have three hundred bucks. Why would I have three hundred bucks?

DAISY: Maybe from your scholarship.

NOAH: They don't give you cash. It just covers board and school fees. I don't have piles of money stashed under my mattress.

DAISY: Then why do you always have nice stuff, like, like your Xbox, and those Converse, and your headphones and stuff?

JIMMY: Yeah, Noah, how *do* you get money for all that stuff?

NOAH: I'm not giving you three hundred bucks. I don't have three hundred bucks. And if I did have three hundred bucks, wouldn't be giving it t'you.

DAISY: Pleeeeeeeeeeeeeeease, Noah, I need money for Gaga tickets.

JIMMY: You can watch the concert on TV, ya know?

DAISY: I have to go in person. It's like, a soul mission that's been implanted into my brain and if I don't go then I'll spontaneously combust.

NOAH: You could ask Dad? He's heaps guilty. I bet you if you called him and cried about missing him and having abandonment issues or whatever he'd transfer you like thirty bucks. Maybe fifty since it's ya birthday.

DAISY: I'm not asking Dad.

NOAH: Why?

DAISY: Because he forgot about my birthday and I never want to hear his dumb voice ever again.

> Pause. NOAH's guilt is palpable.

NOAH: It's easy money, Daze.

> DAISY ignores him.

Who cares about Dad? Just take it.

DAISY: I care, Noah. I have standards.

NOAH: Well, if you can't get three hundred bucks, I guess you'll be watching the concert on TV then.

DAISY: You'll be watching *me* on the TV, Noah, when I meet Lady Gaga, or my name isn't Daisy Moon!

SCENE FIVE

The Woolworths car park.

NOAH *and* JIMMY *sit on milk crates in front of the skips eating a rotisserie chicken from a bag.*

JIMMY: Hey, Tina!

NOAH: Don't call her over.

JIMMY: *Oi! Tina!*

NOAH: I mean it. Haven't talked to her in like a year.

JIMMY: She's full ignoring me. Tina!

> …

Wow, she really hates me. Tina!

> …

Maybe she can't hear me? *Tinaaaaaaaaaa!*

NOAH: She can *definitely* hear you, mate.

JIMMY: Yeah, she hates me.

You know who got fully wet when I mentioned you were in town?

NOAH: Your grandma?

JIMMY: Georgia.

NOAH: Vomit.

JIMMY: What, you prefer my grandma?

NOAH: It would be kinda funny.

JIMMY: No way, Georgia is an absolute babe now. She started doing yoga or whatever and it was like, glasses off, ponytail out, transformation. And she has massive tits. She would definitely bang you if we scored and then took some of it tonight.

NOAH: Not interested.

> PARKER *approaches them.*

PARKER: Howdy, fellas. Do you shop at Woolworths regularly?

> NOAH *and* JIMMY *look* PARKER *up and down, then give each other a look.*

I was wondering if you knew that big retailers are part of the reason we're fishing ourselves into a climate crisis? I have a petition here that might interest you. Do you have a minute to talk about sustainable fishing practices?

JIMMY: I have a minute to talk to you about sustaining my erection. Which you're not.

PARKER: Grow up.

> PARKER *starts walking off.*

JIMMY: [*to* NOAH] If I wanted to chat up a bitch I woulda brought my dog.

PARKER: [*turning back*] Did you say something?

JIMMY: What?

PARKER: Thought you said something to me.

JIMMY: Nah, I didn't say anything.

PARKER: If you have something to say, say it.

NOAH: I don't make a habit of talking to trash.

PARKER: Does your asshole get jealous of the shit that comes out your mouth?

JIMMY: Yikes, she's feisty. Probably on her period.

PARKER: Excuse me?

JIMMY: I asked ya if you're on your *period* because you're acting like a *psycho.*

PARKER: You'll be the one pissing blood if you ask me that again.

NOAH: / Woahhhhh!

JIMMY: Rank! Better get to Woolies before it shuts. Need to stock up on maxi-pads.

PARKER: Excuse me, gentlemen, I need to go buy some *tampons*, because I'm a *woman* now, and you two are obviously boys.

   PARKER *exits.*

JIMMY: What's with these randoms filling up our beaches every summer. Don't give a toss who the locals are. Zero respect.

NOAH: Don't remember it being so touristy.

JIMMY: Better get used to it. Every other house is a bloody Airbnb now.

NOAH: You know, Jimmy, you don't have to 'get used' to anything. Putting up with the status quo is just another way of accepting your mediocrity.

JIMMY: Alright, Einstein, figure of speech.

NOAH: Speaking like that is how people with no dreams talk. That's how Dad talks.

JIMMY: I like your dad.

NOAH: He's an embarrassment.

JIMMY: Least he's not in jail.

NOAH: High school dropout. Married his first girlfriend. Knocked Mum up before high school finished. Still working at the same construction company for twenty years and living in some shitty rental down south.

JIMMY: What's wrong with workin' at the same job? Least he has a job. You're looking at it all wrong. He's living the dream, mate. Pretty much accomplished what everyone everywhere wants.

NOAH: Not me.

JIMMY: Then why not skip town if it's so shit?

   Silence.

NOAH: Dad won't pay my fees without a scholarship, so it's like, fuck him. What the fuck am I supposed to do now?

JIMMY: Start over, I guess.

NOAH: I don't want to start over. I want my old life back.

> *Silence.*

JIMMY: You got any more pills?

> NOAH *hands* JIMMY *the bottle of prescription medication.*

Cheers, Alex, ya mysterious spaz.

NOAH: Alex was my dorm mate at the college. I was selling his Ritalin to students to help 'em study.

JIMMY: Help 'em study?

NOAH: Helps 'em pull all-nighters.

JIMMY: Wait wait wait. Kids give you their *money*, so they can buy *drugs*, to *study*?

NOAH: A lotta kids.

JIMMY: What dumbass kid's gonna waste his hard-earned drug money on studying?

NOAH: It ain't hard-earned. It's trust fund. And pretty much all of 'em.

JIMMY: Shit, man.

NOAH: Yep.

JIMMY: Different world.

> JIMMY *takes another pill then hands the bottle back to* NOAH. NOAH *reads the label, then pockets it.*
>
> *Silence.*
>
> NOAH *stares out to the ocean, breathes in the sea salt breeze.*

NOAH: Ocean smells good.

JIMMY: Better than chlorine.

NOAH: Way better than chlorine.

JIMMY: Welcome home, brother. This is where you belong.

SCENE SIX

The pool tuckshop.

PARKER *wears her work uniform, a retro pinafore with thick pink and white candy-cane stripes over a polo top. Two baseball caps with novelty-sized soft-serve swirls on top, sit on the counter.*

PARKER *reads from an employee manual as she shows* DAISY *around.*

PARKER: So you need to soak the nozzles in bicarb soda overnight. Otherwise they build up a crust and the soft serve comes out crusty. That's the deep fryer. If you're last to finish, you gotta clean out the drip trays. Careful not to spill any grease, or your skin will smell like lard for a literal week. And one of us has to mop the change rooms daily because the shower scum gets heaps slippery. Also the high school girls throw wet paper towels up onto the ceiling and it sticks to the roof. So if that happens you gotta climb up onto the toilet to scrape it off.

DAISY: Got it.

PARKER: Any questions?

DAISY: What if we run out of ice cream?

PARKER: You won't.

DAISY: What if I do?

PARKER: Then say, 'Sorry we're all out'.

DAISY: Oh, just like that? 'Sorry, we're all out.'

PARKER: Sounds perfect.

DAISY: That's easy enough. What do I do if someone wants a refund?

PARKER: Hmmm. I dunno. That's never happened.

DAISY: What do I do if I find a dead bush rat in the deep fryer? And someone sees. And then literally everyone at the pool wants a refund?

PARKER: That will never happen. But I guess you would give them a refund.

DAISY: Cool, just checking. What do I do if someone wees in the pool?

PARKER: That's not our problem, that's the lifeguard's problem. Her name is Emma.

DAISY: What do I do if someone takes a shit in the pool?

PARKER: Why would you think of that?

DAISY: It could happen.

PARKER: Nothing crazy like that has ever happened.

DAISY: Would that be Emma's problem? Or my problem?

PARKER: I reckon Emma's problem.

DAISY: Okay, good.

PARKER: Actually, last week Emma saw this couple, like, full-on doing it in the change rooms. Not even in the toilet cubicle. Literally going for it on the benches.

DAISY: Nice.

PARKER: So I guess some crazy things have happened.

> *Pause.*

Oh, did Gran tell you 'bout the cleaners?

DAISY: No?

PARKER Yeah, she thinks the new cleaners are slacking. So at the start of the day before any customers arrive, you gotta inspect the toilets immediately. And if there's even a speck of shit on the toilet bowl, you gotta document it.

DAISY: Document it?

PARKER: Take a photo on your phone, and text it to my gran.

DAISY: Okay. … I can do that.

PARKER: Oh my God, I'm totally kidding!

DAISY: Oh my God, Parker—

PARKER: Your face! I totally should have let you go hunting for toilet smears.

DAISY: I fully would have!

PARKER: *Ha!* You're so easy.

DAISY: How long have you been working here?

PARKER: Two weeks. Memorised the employee manual on day two.

DAISY: How come you haven't been here any other summer?

PARKER: We move around a lot. I've lived in twenty-one cities in fifteen years.

DAISY: Woah.

PARKER: I'm a global citizen. Normally I go to summer camp so I don't go stir crazy in the compound. Last year was NASA Space Camp, year before surf life saving, year before that soccer, year before that snowboarding—

DAISY: You must know heaps about stuff.

PARKER: Reckon I do.

DAISY: Can I ask you somethin'?

PARKER: Yep.

DAISY: Does your mum have big tits?

PARKER: What?

DAISY: Mine doesn't. And I don't have any either.

PARKER: Oh. Some of the girls at my last school had big ones, even though their mums didn't.

DAISY: So maybe there's still hope.

PARKER: Maybe.

DAISY: You got your period yet?

PARKER: Yeah. You?

DAISY: Yep. When I was twelve. You?

PARKER: Thirteen. And here's your uniform.

PARKER *holds up the two soft-serve caps from the counter.*

DAISY: No way. No *way*.

PARKER: [*putting on a cap*] What, you don't like it?

DAISY: Absolutely not.

PARKER: Overruled. Part of the employment conditions. It's in the manual.

PARKER *shoves the pinafore and polo top into* DAISY's *arms.*

DAISY: You said I could wear whatever I like.

PARKER: I literally never said that.

DAISY: [*putting a cap on her head*] Someone from school might see.

PARKER: So what? I'm wearing it too. You can get changed in the showers. Oh, and no jewellery. So you gotta take off those bangles.

DAISY: You mean my glow sticks?

PARKER: Is that what they are?

DAISY: Well, they don't glow anymore because they're real old.

PARKER: Well, you gotta take 'em off. 'No jewellery'. It's in the employee manual.

DAISY: But I always wear them.

NOAH *enters, ready to start training for the day.*

NOAH: What are you wearing?

DAISY: What does it look like?

NOAH: It looks like My Little Pony took a shit on your head.

PARKER: You know him?

DAISY: Parker, meet my butthead brother, Noah.

PARKER: We've met.

DAISY: Where were you last night? You missed cake.

NOAH: Beach.

DAISY: Mum was worried.

NOAH: Didn't text or nothing.

DAISY: I texted you.

NOAH: So?

DAISY: You look like hell.

NOAH: You can talk.

DAISY: Your eyes are all bloodshot.

NOAH: It's the chlorine. Do you work here now?

DAISY: Yes.

NOAH: With her?

DAISY: Yes.

NOAH: And that's your uniform?

DAISY: …

NOAH: Well, that's embarrassing.

DAISY: Yes, Noah, this is my *embarrassing work uniform* because I am a *responsible* member of society who goes to *work* and doesn't stay out all night because I have a summer job.

> DAISY *exits to the change rooms with her chin held high.*
>
> NOAH *and* PARKER *eyeball each other. Decide not to speak.*
>
> *Awkward silence.*

NOAH: You're friends with Daisy? Same school or something?

PARKER: In town for summer.

NOAH: Tourist.

PARKER: I don't make a habit of talking to trash.

NOAH: Yeah. Sorry 'bout that, we were just messing.

PARKER: Sure you were.

NOAH: I didn't mean anything by it.

PARKER: So it's just a fun little hobby of yours to sexually harass strangers?

NOAH: …

PARKER: Thought so.

NOAH: Fair call. Will you accept a genuine apology?

PARKER: Pool entry's three bucks.

NOAH: I'm serious. I think what you're doing with the petition and stuff is … cool.

PARKER: I honestly don't care what you think.

NOAH: It takes guts. And I respect that.

PARKER: Well, standing up to the bullies of the world isn't fun or easy, but someone's gotta do it.

NOAH: Yeah.

PARKER: You don't need to humour me.

NOAH: Nah, I agree. Can't let anyone think they're untouchable, or they'll really start to believe it, right?

PARKER: Right.

Pause.

So you wanna sign the petition? I'm delivering it to the Woolworths store manager as soon as I get two hundred signatures.

NOAH: How many you got now?

PARKER: Let's just say yours will take me into double digits.

PARKER *gets the petition and hands* NOAH *the clipboard.*

So it's name, date of birth, and email address.

NOAH: Wait wait wait, I see what you're doing. This is just an elaborate excuse to get my email. You know you can just ask me?

PARKER: Let me guess. Douche dot bag at jerk-face dot com?

NOAH: Try super hot swimming champion at standing right in front of you dot com.

PARKER: …

NOAH: C'mon. That was a good one.

PARKER: …

NOAH: Admit it. It was pretty funny.

PARKER: Pool entry's three bucks. You wanna swim, it's three bucks.

NOAH: Am I not good enough for you or something? Is that it?

PARKER: Yes, that's definitely 'it'.

NOAH: You reckon you know something 'bout this town, do ya? You been here what, a week?

PARKER: I know that the local economy relies on jobs created by the aquaculture industry. And fishing is what keeps half of this community out of poverty. And that making more and more of Australia's oceans protected marine parks puts locals out of work. Which creates the perfect melting pot for exploitation. So yeah, dickhead, I know something about it.

Pause.

NOAH: Alright, gimme a pen.

PARKER *passes him a pen.*

[*Signing the petition*] Not that one signature's gonna make a difference.

PARKER: I think it can.

> NOAH *hands her back the clipboard.*

NOAH: Look, some institutions, some businesses, some people *are* untouchable. It sucks, and it's shitty and it's unfair, but it's true. You're wasting ya time tryin' t' fight 'em.

> DAISY *enters.*

DAISY: [*twirling*] Ta-da! Lady Gaga, here I come!

NOAH: Maybe you'll actually make it inside the stadium this time.

DAISY: Screw you.

NOAH: Too soon?

PARKER: What?

DAISY: I had tickets last tour, but … plans changed.

PARKER: How come?

DAISY: …

> *An awkward silence.*

NOAH: Yeah, I'm not gonna do this.

> NOAH *goes to enter the pool area.*

DAISY: Mum said you have to mow the lawn this arvo.

NOAH: Can't. Going to a party.

DAISY: You were out last night.

NOAH: Yeah, and I'm going out again tonight. You going?

DAISY: Whose party?

NOAH: Georgia's.

DAISY: Georgia's the worst.

NOAH: You not friends anymore?

DAISY: Not anymore.

NOAH: Surprise, surprise, Daisy making no effort to fit in.

DAISY: Fit in with your shallow friends? No thank you.

NOAH: At least I have friends.

DAISY: At least I have fucking standards!

NOAH: Woah, no-one respects a foul mouth, Daisy.

DAISY: Well, I don't respect a cheat.

PARKER: Anyway!

> [*To* NOAH] Pool entry's three bucks.
>
> [*To* DAISY] Daisy, I'll show you how to use the till.

NOAH: Wait up—what's on ya shorts?

PARKER: [*checking herself*] What?

NOAH: No, on Daisy, there's something on the back of your—

DAISY: What?

> DAISY *turns around. Blood has soaked through the back of her work pinafore. She got her first period.*

Oh my God.

NOAH: That's rank!

DAISY: I musta sat in something!

NOAH: You got ya rags!

DAISY: No I didn't.

NOAH: It's all over your uniform!

DAISY: Shut up, Noah!

PARKER: Give her your hoodie—

NOAH: What? Why?

PARKER: To tie round her waist.

NOAH: No way!

DAISY: I'm not workin' all day with nothin' but a hoodie hiding it.

PARKER: Seriously, no-one will see, it's fine.

NOAH: *Everyone* will see that murder scene.

DAISY: Can I get a new uniform?

PARKER: Totally! Der, why didn't I think of that? Daisy, watch the till.

DAISY: No, wait, Parker—

PARKER: [*exiting*] I'll be sixty seconds.

DAISY: [*groaning to herself*] Oh my God.

Alright, Daisy's a loser, you've had ya laugh.

NOAH: Why'd ya call me a cheat in front of ya friend?

DAISY: …

NOAH: You don't know anything 'bout what happened, alright? So that's strike two. And if you go spewin' ya mouth off again / I swear—

DAISY: Oh, boo-fucking-hoo, Noah! If you weren't so obsessed with your precious reputation—

NOAH: I don't need you intentionally trying to ruin my year.

DAISY: I don't give a flip what kinda year you have. It's not like you gave a shit about me this year, which was actually the *worst* year of my life.

NOAH: I know.

DAISY: If you *knew*, then why didn't you call or message me or anything?

NOAH: I was busy. Training got really intense

DAISY: That musta been real hard for you. Way, way harder than living at home after Dad left. Because in case you were wondering, Mum's a total zombie now and everything's completely shit.

Long pause.

NOAH: Well …

I'm stuck here now so …

If you wanna talk?

DAISY: I don't *want* to talk to you anymore, okay. I've moved on.

NOAH: I'm being serious.

DAISY: This is rank. I'm leavin'.

NOAH: Just wait a minute and get a new uniform.

DAISY: Don't tell me what to do!

NOAH: Chill out, ya psycho.

DAISY: I'm going home.

NOAH: Daisy, don't be dumb, you can't walk out on your shift.

DAISY: Yes I can. I quit.

PARKER *enters holding a pair of old sweatpants.*

PARKER: [*entering*] Found some trackies in lost property!

DAISY: Forget it, I'm outta here.

NOAH: Daisy, stop, why would you do that?

DAISY: Dunno, Noah, quitting must run in the family.

DAISY *exits.*

Long pause.

NOAH: Please don't fire her. I know she seems freaking weird, but she's usually really normal … and, um … reliable.

Yep. Gold star employee for sure.

And sorry about calling you a trash yesterday.

I assumed I'd never see you again.

Yet here we are.

…

Awkward.

PARKER: Please leave.

SCENE SEVEN

The bus stop on Daisy Moon's front lawn.

DAISY: Gaga? Gaga! It's me Daisy, your number one fan!
Hello?
I became a woman today, in case you were wondering.
Hellooooooooo?

DAISY *slumps on the bus stop bench, pulls her knees to her chest, squeezes her eyes tightly shut, takes a deep breath.*

Dear Gaga, if you're listening right now it's super important you tell me how the heck I'm meant to get to your concert.

GAGA: Greetings Earthling. Mother Monster can't tune into your frequency right now. So leave your psychic vibrations after the tone and I'll get back to you when feel like it. Beeeeeeeeeep.

DAISY: Gaga. It's me, Daisy! Call me back, okay, I really need someone to talk to.

PARKER *enters.*

PARKER: Daisy?

DAISY: [*opening her eyes*] Gaga? Oh. Parker.
Didn't you hear me, I quit, alright.

PARKER: Here's your cut of the tip jar.

PARKER *gives* DAISY *sixty-cents.*

DAISY: Shrapnel. Thanks.

PARKER: You lasted twenty-five minutes.

DAISY: I'll never afford tickets.

PARKER: Well, if you see me at the pool tomorrow we can pretend today never happened.

DAISY: Why would you let me come back?

PARKER: I think people deserve second chances.

DAISY: Just like that?

PARKER: Just like that.

PARKER *looks around at the DIY posters on the bus shelter walls. She pauses to trace her fingers along a 'Monster Ball' tour poster.*

DAISY: Mum painted that one.

PARKER: Woah. I legit thought it was a real poster.

DAISY: It is a real poster.

PARKER: I mean from a concert.

DAISY: Oh.

My glow sticks are from a concert. Look. Lady Gaga official merchandise.

PARKER: So you've seen her in person?

DAISY: Nah.

PARKER: Then how'd you get the glow sticks?

DAISY: Mum was meant to take me but, um, she didn't get outta bed that morning. So I asked Dad, but Noah had a Country Squad meet that weekend, and Dad had to drive Noah to Bega. Noah totally could have skipped one meet, but he freaking guilted Dad like crazy. So I begged and begged Mum until she caved. Which turned out to be a rubbish idea because she had a total meltdown at the stadium gates, and the St John's Ambulance dudes said we couldn't go inside.

Pause.

PARKER: She seemed nice in your kitchen this morning.

DAISY: Yeah, because she was performing 'normal', which she isn't.

PARKER: …

DAISY: I mean, it's not like those weird depression commercials with lame symbolism like dark grey shadows and waves crashing on rocks. She's just really, really super sad all the time. Doesn't get out of bed. Doesn't paint anymore. Doesn't brush her hair. Doesn't do anything she used to do.

Pause.

PARKER: What's your favourite song to listen to when you're sad?

DAISY: 'Marry the Night'.

PARKER: I got the 'Born This Way' album for my birthday.

DAISY: Me too! When's your birthday?

PARKER: March twenty-eight.

A magical chiming sound.

DAISY: The same as Gaga's.

PARKER: What?

DAISY: You have the *exact same birthday* as Lady Gaga!

PARKER: No way.

DAISY: For freaking *real*!

PARKER: Stop looking at me funny.

DAISY: I'm not.

PARKER: You are.

DAISY: Are you real?

PARKER: What the heck, yes I'm real.

DAISY: Prove it.

PARKER: How?

DAISY: Can I pinch you?

PARKER: 'Kay, but that's not how it works.

DAISY: Gimme ya arm.

> PARKER *lifts up her sleeve.* DAISY *pinches her skin.*

Hmmm.

PARKER: Pinch harder.

DAISY: [*pinching harder*] Doesn't that hurt?

PARKER: Nah, feels nice.

DAISY: Definitely alien. Try reading my mind.

PARKER: How?

> DAISY *takes* PARKER's *hands and holds them to her cheeks.* DAISY *stares very intensely into* PARKER's *eyes.*

DAISY: Read. My. Mind. And. *Go!*

PARKER: You're full mental.

DAISY: That's what Noah reckons.

PARKER: Yeah. But, I mean it in a good way.

DAISY: For real?

PARKER: Yep.

DAISY: Who wants t'be normal anyway?

> PARKER *releases* DAISY.

PARKER: So when's the next one?

DAISY: Next what?

PARKER: Monster Meeting.

DAISY: Um, it's supposed to be right about now. But the guest of honour didn't show up today.

PARKER: Who's that?

DAISY: Never mind.

PARKER: Guess I should leave you to it.

DAISY: You're leaving?

PARKER: Since my temporary membership expired after twenty-four hours.

DAISY: You can join for real if you like?

PARKER: I'm fresh outta tenners.

DAISY: Mademoiselle Parker, as President and Founder of the Batemans Bay Little Monsters Fan club, I would be truly honoured if you would join as a *lifetime* member.

PARKER: [*teasing*] I dunnnoooooo …

DAISY: I mean it. I'll make you Vice-President. Maybe the reason why at this precise moment in space and time you stayed at your gran's for summer, is so you can become a Little Monster. It's time to answer that call, Parker.

PARKER: Alright, I'll join.

DAISY: We're technically a fan club, but it's more of a music appreciation society, to be accurate.

PARKER: Right.

DAISY: Members meet here every day during summer. We're going through a dry spell. It's actually just me at the moment. And now you. So that's a one hundred percent increase in memberships in the last two minutes alone. Monsters Meetings are a combination of philosophical debates, dance rehearsals and crafter-noons. We're exceptionally creative. I made my troll crown at the last meeting.

PARKER: I wish I could make stuff.

DAISY: Magic like this doesn't happen overnight.

> DAISY *stands on the bus stop bench.*

[*Clearing her throat*] Ah-hem! As President of the Batemans Bay Little Monsters Fan Club I now call our congregation to session. First up, I would like to welcome our newest monster, Mademoiselle Parker! Welcome, star sister. The focus of today's meeting will be on validation and loving ourselves. Little Monsters accept that we, just as we are, are truly marvelous. So, we're going to go around the … circle … and list all the reasons why we're special. I'll go first. I'm special because …

Um.

Because …

I'm President!

Now you.

PARKER: Okay. I'm special because I'm Vice-President.

DAISY: I'm special because …

I'm special because …

I got nothing.

Pause.

PARKER: You became a woman today.

DAISY: Yeah.

PARKER: Was that your first?

DAISY: Maybe.

PARKER: Why'd you lie 'bout it?

DAISY: Wanted you to like me.

Pause.

PARKER: I'm special because when I move towns, I can forget people ever existed.

DAISY: Really?

PARKER: Yep.

DAISY *considers* PARKER*'s answer. After a moment …*

DAISY: I'm special because when people leave, I still love them.

The girls sit in silence, staring out at the ocean.

END OF ACT ONE

ACT TWO

The pool tuckshop.

DAISY *and* PARKER *are hard at work.* *Both girls wear their work uniforms, though* DAISY *has slightly pimped hers with gemstones spelling out 'D-Moon' across the back of her polo shirt.* *Their familiarity with the space should indicate that time has passed.*

JIMMY *enters.*

JIMMY: You seen Noah?

PARKER: Still training.

JIMMY: Still?

PARKER: Till four I think.

JIMMY: It's ten past.

PARKER: Then I guess he's done.

JIMMY: Sweet, I'll go meet him.

DAISY: Pool entry's three bucks. You wanna find Noah, you gotta pay.

JIMMY: I'm just stickin' my head round the corner.

DAISY: Ah-ah-ah, you cross this yellow line, you gotta pay entry.

JIMMY: You for real?

DAISY: You're getting awfully close to the line, buster.

JIMMY: Oi, Noah!

    Oi! Noah!

PARKER: Stop / yelling!

JIMMY: Noahhhhhhh!

    Whatever.

    I gotta piss anyways.

DAISY: You wanna piss? It's still three bucks.

JIMMY: Since when is this place run like a Westfield.

PARKER: Three bucks, Jimmy, you got it or not?

JIMMY: Guess I'll have ta go right here.

    JIMMY *starts to drop his pants.*

PARKER: / No! Just go in!

DAISY: What the flip, stop! Fine, go through!

PARKER: Toilets are through and on the left.

JIMMY: I know where they are. I've been coming here my whole life, tourist.

Tell Noah when you see him I'm waiting for him out front.

[*Tipping his cap to them as he exits*] Ladies.

DAISY *and* PARKER *perform a sequence of tasks in perfect synchronisation. Unpacking a delivery box, throwing items to one another, building the perfect snack pyramid.* DAISY *notices a pool patron.*

DAISY: [*pointing*] Southern Cross tattoo at three o'clock!

PARKER: Where?

DAISY: By the wheelie bins.

PARKER: Can't see it.

DAISY: On his shoulder. Wait, he's turned around.

Wait for it …

Wait for it …

There!

PARKER: Oh, it's on.

A familiar game of customer bingo between them begins. The girls grab their DIY scorecards. They scan the horizon.

DAISY: Dirty Band-Aid floating in the pool!

PARKER: Don't see it.

DAISY: Baby pool.

PARKER: Dammit.

DAISY: That's Daisy: two. Parker: zero.

PARKER: Australian flag board shorts.

DAISY: Crocs and socks.

PARKER: C'mon, c'mon, G-string tan line.

DAISY: Oooooo, rat's tail on a four-year-old.

PARKER: Hairy belly wearing Speedos.

DAISY: Where?

PARKER: Exiting the showers. That's one, two, in a row—

DAISY: *No!* Wait! G-string tan line!

PARKER: Where?

DAISY: On the deckchairs. That's one, two, three in a row—

PARKER: Noooo—

DAISY: *Bingo!* Ha-ha, yes. Looks like you're mopping the showers.

Pause.

PARKER: You cool if we swap shifts, and you close up today?

DAISY: You would trust me with such sacred duties as degreasing the deep fryer and hosing down the shower scum?

PARKER: I see you've read the employee manual.

DAISY: You've taught me well.

PARKER: So you're cool?

DAISY: Yep. Ya helping ya gran or something?

PARKER: Gonna go exploring round the river.

DAISY: Oh, it's heaps nice there. I use t'go there all the time as a kid. Me 'n' Noah'd play in the rock pools.

PARKER: Yeah. Noah suggested it.

DAISY: Noah?

PARKER: At the bus stop this morning.

NOAH *enters.*

DAISY: Jimmy's lookin' for ya.

NOAH: I'm so freaking over these water-boy chores.

DAISY: Suck it up and do 'em anyway. It's worth it to train for free.

NOAH: It's humiliating.

DAISY: Get over yourself, no-one's judging you.

NOAH: They are.

PARKER: I'm not.

NOAH: I should be the priority. Not unlocking change rooms and collecting wet towels.

DAISY: [*to* PARKER] Noah's paranoid the coach's got something against him.

NOAH: He does. He's intimidated. Look how the club's doing under his leadership.

PARKER: Um, bad? Is the answer bad?

NOAH: Financially, rubbish. Which he knows I know. I mean, facilities aside, funding wise it's a freaking nightmare, since the club can never hold onto its main talent. Coach said, 'You're so blessed to have your talent, Noah. So lucky.'

DAISY: That's a *nice* thing to say.

NOAH: Has nothing to do with luck. Sports is about hard work and discipline and sacrifice. Calling it luck is such an insult.

DAISY: You know what I'd do if I were you, Noah.

NOAH: I don't want your opinion, Daisy. I'm just venting for a minute—

DAISY: I'd start my own swim team.

NOAH: Please don't give me advice—

DAISY: You can call it Team Noah. Or Noah's Ark. Or Moon Squad! And you can coach yourself. And you wouldn't need funding. You could raise money by holding a sausage sizzle at Bunnings. And you can make your own way to Nationals. Everyone would *love* that. You'd become a local hero.

NOAH: I'm banned from competing, Daisy.

DAISY: I'm being optimistic.

NOAH: There's no Nationals, alright. It's over.

Awkward silence. NOAH *fiddles with the stopwatch around his neck.*

Stopwatch's busted.

…

So times this morning are totally useless.

PARKER: Show me.

NOAH *shows* PARKER.

NOAH: When I double click this button instead of tracking lap times, it completely resets.

PARKER: Woah, what's with your hands?

NOAH: What? Oh, yeah, I spend so much time in the water that my fingers are totally messed. The skin's like permanently shrivelled.

PARKER: [*touching his hand*] It's all bumpy.

DAISY *stares uncomfortably at the floor.*

NOAH: Skin peels off in chunks all the time and, anyways, it's rank.

PARKER: Feels nice.

DAISY: Jimmy's looking for you, Noah. He's right out front.

NOAH: [*to* PARKER] So there's a thing next Saturday.

PARKER: What?

NOAH: Never mind

PARKER: Tell me.

NOAH: There's a thing. But you probably wouldn't wanna go?

PARKER: I might.

DAISY: What *thing?* Get your own friends, Noah.

NOAH: New Year's Eve party.

PARKER: Yeah, looks heaps fun.

NOAH: You going? Everyone goes. It's like a thing around here. Massive bonfire. All the local kids go. You should go.

DAISY: We got something better to do.

NOAH: Better than a bonfire?

PARKER: She's not lying, we do have something better.

DAISY and PARKER: [*together*] Lady Gaga concert!

DAISY: It's the same night.

PARKER: Daisy and I are getting tickets tomorrow.

DAISY: Lining up early.

NOAH: So Daisy Moon managed to save three hundred bucks?

DAISY: Ding ding ding!

> NOAH *raises his hand to high-five* DAISY.

NOAH: Nice one, little sis.

DAISY: [*high-fiving* NOAH] Yewwww!

> PARKER *puts on her backpack.*

NOAH: [*to* PARKER] You all good to go?

PARKER: Yep. Daisy's closing up.

NOAH: Sweet.

PARKER: [*to* DAISY] See you tomorrow?

DAISY: Where you two going?

PARKER: Noah's showing me where the creek is.

DAISY: Under the main bridge where the river splits.

> *Long pause.*

PARKER: … Cool.

Thanks.

So I'll see you tomorrow, Daisy?

> NOAH *and* PARKER *start to leave.*

[*Exiting*] Lining up at six, right?

NOAH: [*exiting*] See ya.

DAISY: You haven't mopped the showers.

PARKER: [*turning back*] What?

DAISY: You lost bingo; you have to mop the showers. That's the rules of the game.

Pause.

NOAH: Can't you do it?

DAISY: But I won.

Pause.

PARKER: I'll go do it now. Meet you out front, Noah?

NOAH: Yep.

NOAH *exits to the front of the pool where* JIMMY *is waiting.*

PARKER *grabs a mop and bucket and exits to the showers.*

DAISY *continues the task from earlier but without* PARKER. *It's less coordinated without the pair of them.*

NOAH *and* JIMMY *are out the front out of earshot from* DAISY, *the scene outside continues.*

JIMMY: Been waitin' for ya. C'mon, we're going.

NOAH: Where?

JIMMY: The pier. Listen, I've been thinking. You got the brawns, but I got the brains. Abalone!

NOAH: …

JIMMY: Abalone diving. As a job. It's seasonal, so it's seventy working days a year and that's it. You're on a boat. In the water. Seventy days, then ya done. See ya next season. Wait till ya hear how much it pays.

NOAH: Not interested.

JIMMY: One hundred K.

NOAH: Shit.

JIMMY: I'm doing it, man. I'm getting my commercial diving licence.

NOAH: What about school?

JIMMY: One *hundred* K. One hundred *thousand* dollars for seventy days work.

NOAH: For real?

JIMMY: Listen, they need strong swimmers. You're in underwater for six hours at a time. Heaps a' people aren't cut out for it. Bosses would froth at the mouth for a guy like you.

NOAH: Ya reckon?

JIMMY: Young, check. Fit, check. Ex-Olympic athlete, check check.

NOAH: I was never Olympic level—

JIMMY: You're a good swimmer and this way you can still swim.

NOAH: …

   I got plans this afternoon.

JIMMY: Doing what?

NOAH: …

   Just stuff.

JIMMY: Just hear what he has to say.

NOAH: I said I have plans.

JIMMY: Noah, I told him 'bout you. I said my best mate's Olympic-level good. He was real keen. I said we're joined at the hip, best mates, and we come as a pair. He wants t' meet ya.

NOAH: …

JIMMY: Come on, I need this.

NOAH: I didn't ask you to do that.

JIMMY: You're gonna bail on your best friend?

NOAH: … Sorry, Jimmy. Not today, alright.

JIMMY: I'm trying to hook up a job. I have something to lose by blowing them off.

NOAH: I have things to lose—

JIMMY: No you don't. You have nothing to lose because you don't actually have anything. No scholarship, no job, no swimming career, no nothing. You have no skills, other than the fact that you can swim. And guess what, no-one in the real world gives a fuck. So don't bail on me here.

NOAH: Well, last time I checked they don't give out trophies for 'not bailing'.

JIMMY: Who gives a shit about trophies? I'm trying to help you out.

NOAH: You're the last person I'd ask for help.

JIMMY: What's that s'posed t' mean?

NOAH: It means it feels like ya helping yourself. Not me.

JIMMY: This'll work out for the both of us.

NOAH: I'm not gonna let you ride my coat-tails. I worked really hard for what I achieved.

JIMMY: Yeah? And guess what? You weren't even good enough. You needed steroids to keep up. So turns out you're no better than the rest of us.

NOAH: Okay, here's my prediction of how your plan'll play out.

JIMMY: Go for it.

NOAH: You'll fail your commercial diver's licence exam because you have no respect for the strength it takes to be underwater for six hours at a time. So you'll get some other job, it'll probably be a shitty job, and you'll probably suck at it, and you'll probably get fired, so you'll just get another shitty job. And you'll keep bouncing from shitty job to shitty job because you're always looking for a shortcut.

Long pause.

JIMMY: Is that really what ya think of me?

NOAH: …

JIMMY: I fucking take ya back after what you did and this is how ya treat people now?

Long pause. They stare at each other.

Whatever.

JIMMY *leaves.*

NOAH *sits down, frustrated, waiting for* PARKER.

PARKER *enters the tuckshop where* DAISY *is.*

PARKER: Hey, are any of the lifeguards still around?

DAISY: Emma's gone home for the day.

PARKER: So that means you'll be the last one leaving?

DAISY: Yep.

PARKER: You know what, don't worry about Noah, I'm gonna stay late with you.

DAISY: Just go, Parker, not like I give a shit.

PARKER: I'll check out the creek some other time.

DAISY: So you like Noah now?

PARKER: No.

DAISY: Don't go there, he's a mess.

PARKER: He seems nice.

DAISY: He's not.

PARKER: He seems normal.

DAISY: Since when do we like normal?

Long pause.

Just go, I don't give a shit.

PARKER: Fine. But I'm still gonna do the showers. I couldn't get them cleaned up, but I'll come in early and finish tomorrow morning.

DAISY: Whatever.

PARKER: Promise me you won't do it for me, okay?

> DAISY *ignores her. Begins counting the tips in the tip jar, dividing them in two piles for her and* PARKER.

I locked them up so no-one can go in. They can just use the disabled ones. Promise you'll let me finish tomorrow? After we buy concert tickets.

DAISY: Fine!

PARKER: I'll come in early—

DAISY: I said fine!

> *Pause.*

PARKER: See you later.

> PARKER *puts the keys to the showers in a drawer and leaves. She meets* NOAH *out front and the pair exit together.*

> DAISY, *still inside the tuckshop, slumps over the counter. She scoops her pile of tips into her pinafore pocket.*

> *After a moment she decides to take Parker's tips as well.*

> *After a moment she feels guilty and puts Parker's half back in the tip jar.*

> *She stands alone, surveying the pool.*

> *She opens the drawer and takes out the keys to the showers. Stares at the keys in her hands.*

SCENE NINE

The creek.

NOAH *and* PARKER *walk along the top of the rocks that join the creek to the bush scrub.*

NOAH *searches the trees on the opposite side of the creek to* PARKER.

PARKER: [*calling out to him from across the creek*] Do you like swimming?

NOAH: Found it!

PARKER: And do you like it coz you're good at it, or coz you actually enjoy doing it?

NOAH: Right next to this rock.

PARKER: Or do you not like it at all, but you're good at it, so you keep doing it?

NOAH: What's that even matter?

PARKER: Changes everything, depending on your answer.

NOAH: [*indicating an old gum tree*] Look. 'N.M. loves G.D.'

> PARKER *joins* NOAH.

PARKER: G.D.?

NOAH: Georgia Dixon. Daisy's best friend.

PARKER: *Georgia* Georgia?

NOAH: Yeah.

PARKER: Daisy hates Georgia.

> NOAH *shrugs.*

NOAH: Was obsessed with her when I was ten. Spent two hours carving our initials into this tree. Jimmy gave me heaps for it. Told me girls were gross.

PARKER: Was she your girlfriend?

NOAH: First love yes. Girlfriend no.

PARKER: Second love?

NOAH: The pool.

PARKER: Third love?

> NOAH *considers, then answers honestly.*

NOAH: Nothing.

PARKER: You still train, though.

> *Pause.*

NOAH: When I was little I was heaps scared of water.

PARKER: For real?

NOAH: One time I slipped into the creek right up round that bend there, and Daisy jumped in and pulled me out. Makes zero sense, she was so tiny, but people can do mental things in a crisis, ay? 'Specially if you love 'em. Mum put me into lessons after that and, yeah, took to it I guess.

> *Silence.*

So this is the spot I was telling you 'bout.

PARKER: Better than the chicken shop.

NOAH: What you plan on doing here all afternoon?

PARKER: Read a book or somethin'.

NOAH: Didn't ya hear? No-one reads books anymore.

PARKER: Found one of Gran's.

> PARKER *takes a book from her backpack and passes it to* NOAH.

NOAH: Palmistry?

PARKER: *The Ancient Alchemy of Palmistry.* This is some seriously heavy stuff.

NOAH: Lame.

PARKER: Gran read my palm five summers ago, and literally *everything* came true.

NOAH: I'm sure it had nothing to do with coincidence.

PARKER: *Everythingggggg—*

NOAH: Stop messing.

PARKER: I'm serious. Learned to ride a bike that summer. Broke my arm. Had my first pash. And it was all there in my life line. Do you think fate's real?

NOAH: Nah.

PARKER: Not even a little bit?

NOAH: Maybe karma. Reckon karma's real. But nah, not fate.

PARKER: I like thinking I've got a destiny.

NOAH: And now it makes sense.

PARKER: What?

NOAH: Why you're friends with Daisy.

PARKER: Yeah, she's cool.

> NOAH *flicks through the palmistry book.*

Okay, gimme your hand.

NOAH: I don't believe in that stuff.

PARKER: I can read your love line.

NOAH: Nup. That shit's creepy.

PARKER: Thought you didn't *believe* in it?

NOAH: You don't have to *believe* in something to find it creepy.

PARKER: Please?

NOAH: Go on then.

> NOAH *gives* PARKER *his hand.*

PARKER: Your other hand.

NOAH: Oh my God—

> PARKER *takes* NOAH*'s hand and traces the lines of his palm with her fingertip.*

PARKER: Okay, this line here that sweeps around your thumb, is your life line.

> And your head line is the straight one here.
>
> And this line above is your heart line.
>
> I think … your heart line is sort of, it's kind of hard to see.

NOAH: Yeah, I told you, my skin's all messed up from the pool.

PARKER: No wait, it's this one here.

NOAH: That's a scar from climbing on some oysters. It's heaps deep, hey?

PARKER: It's your heart line.

NOAH: It's a scar.

PARKER: Fine. No heart line. I'll read your life line.

> Okay, so yours is made up of lots of short little lines. But the grooves are real deep. Hmmm …

> PARKER *checks the book.*

[*Reading*] 'Many breaks in your life line indicates someone of great charm and popularity.'

NOAH: Okay, clearly true.

PARKER: [*reading*] 'Of course, there is a downside to their persuasive nature. They can often find themselves bidding desperately for attention, and are narcissistic to a fault.'

NOAH: Ouch. That's rude.

PARKER: [*reading*] 'They must guard against their tendency to self-sabotage. Be careful you don't lose everything you've built because of a character flaw.'

> PARKER *stares at the book.* NOAH *stares at his palm.*

Wow.

NOAH: …

PARKER: That's weird.

NOAH: …

PARKER: That's actually really weird.

> NOAH *hides his hands in his pockets.*

Don't you think that's weird?

NOAH: Why?

PARKER: You know. The whole … getting expelled situation? Daisy told me 'bout the steroids.

NOAH: Nice.

> *Awkward pause.* PARKER *can sense* NOAH'*s anger, but doesn't know what to say.*

PARKER: This psychic stuff's all made up anyway.

NOAH: I know.

PARKER: It's just pseudo-science—

NOAH: I said I know.

> *Pause.*

PARKER: Sorry.

NOAH: Let's hear yours then.

PARKER: We don't have to.

NOAH: If I have to you have to.

> PARKER *doesn't know what to do so, she continues reading.*

PARKER: Okay. So, should we read my love line? Or … fate?

NOAH: Fate.

PARKER: [*studying her own palm*] Mine's forked. See how all these little lines look like tree branches?

NOAH: Yeah, they kinda do, huh.

PARKER: And the lines are all wispy.

> PARKER *flicks to find the page.*

[*Reading*] 'A forked fate line indicates a traveller. Someone motivated by their urge to explore the world. They are highly romantic and can fall quickly in and out of love with projects and people.' [*Looking up*] Anyway! It goes on.

NOAH: Oh, c'mon. Right before the good stuff. You gotta finish it now.

PARKER: [*reading*] '… they can fall quickly in and out of love with projects and people. However, they are the ultimate outsiders. Living life forever on the fringes.'

NOAH: [*whistling the 'Twilight Zone' theme music*] Do-do-do-do, Do-do-do-do.

PARKER: What?

NOAH: In other words, Tourist with a capital T.

PARKER, *hurt, closes the book.*

What?

PARKER: I'm a global citizen, there's a difference.

NOAH: 'Global citizen'?

PARKER: There's heaps of different places I call home. Including here. This is where my grandparents live.

NOAH: Doesn't make you local.

PARKER, *annoyed, finds a seat away from* NOAH.

Pause.

NOAH *shuffles closer to her and reaches to hold her hand.*

PARKER: [*moving her hand away*] Tourist, so, I'm leaving eventually.

NOAH: Eventually's not now.

PARKER *shrugs.*

You afraid of goodbyes or something?

PARKER: Didn't use to be.

NOAH: Yeah, well … it'd be weird if you weren't.

SCENE TEN

The pool showers.

DAISY *unlocks the door and steps inside. She switches on the lights.*

Graffiti that covers the shower walls reads …
    'Daisy Moon's a dyke'
    'Go kill yourself you fugly slut'
    'Lezzo freak'
    'Povo loser'.

DAISY *stares at the graffiti.*

Silence.

DAISY *frantically begins scrubbing it off.*

SCENE ELEVEN

Noah's bedroom. The early hours of the morning. The room is noticeably more lived-in since Scene Three.

NOAH *sleeps in his bed.* DAISY *knocks anxiously, and then peeks through the door. She enters and stands in the doorway.*

DAISY: Noah?

NOAH: …

DAISY: Hey, Noah?

> DAISY *comes into the room and sits on the end of his bed.*

Noah, you awake?

> NOAH *stirs and rolls over.*

NOAH: Rack off.

DAISY: It's Mum.

NOAH: What?

DAISY: I said it's Mum.

> NOAH *sits up, alert.*

NOAH: Oh shit, is she dead?

DAISY: Nah, but I called the ambos.

NOAH: You called the ambos?

DAISY: They already came and took her.

NOAH: …

DAISY: Aunt Meg's coming to pick us up, and we'll meet 'em in ED. So you gotta get dressed.

NOAH: I'll drive us.

DAISY: Car's been busted for eight months.

NOAH: Fuckin' typical.

> NOAH *gets outta bed. Finds a sweatshirt. Begins getting dressed.*

DAISY: Was meant to head out early to meet Parker, so my alarm was set for four a.m. Went to use the bathroom, the bathroom door was locked so … yeah. Just the usual signs, I guess.

NOAH: I'll tell Dad.

DAISY: He won't come.

NOAH: He'll come.

DAISY: You can call him, but he won't come.

NOAH: He'll fuckin' come, Daisy.

DAISY: …

NOAH: …

DAISY: Fine. Call.

> NOAH *dials. It rings out and through to voicemail.*

NOAH: [*to* DAISY, *covering the receiver*] It's voicemail.
DAISY: Told you.
NOAH: It's early.
DAISY: For a construction worker?
NOAH: [*into the phone*] Hey, Dad ... it's Noah. I know you're 'bout to start work, but, ah, Mum's at the hospital. I dunno, Daisy found her. And the ambos came. Call me back, alright. You should probably come up here for a bit.

> NOAH *hangs up.*

DAISY: Ten bucks he says he didn't get the voicemail.
NOAH: He'll get it after work.
DAISY: He's gonna drive up after work?
NOAH: Yeah, so?
DAISY: He's gonna drive six hours from Lakes Entrance *after* work?
NOAH: ...
DAISY: Probably make Mum worse if he shows.
NOAH: I don't wanna have to deal with this shit on my own, alright?

> *Pause.*

DAISY: Kinda like I had to this year?

> *Pause.*

NOAH: He'll come when he knows it's *actually* really bad.
DAISY: Pretty sure he knows, Noah. Pretty sure you knew too. Didn't mean you called back.
NOAH: ...
DAISY: We're all each other's got now.
NOAH: ...
DAISY: ...
NOAH: I could go live with Dad.
DAISY: As if.
NOAH: I could.

> *Pause.*

Jimmy found work down south. On a commercial fishing boat. I could go if I wanted. Said bosses would jump at a guy like me.
DAISY: ... And just leave again?
NOAH: Maybe.

Long pause.

Oh, come on, don't look at me like that. You gotta look out for yourself, Daisy. You gotta learn how to help yourself, alright, otherwise you'll end up like Mum.

DAISY: That's a really fucking mean thing to say.

NOAH: Well, it's true. She doesn't help herself. The same thing keeps happening again and happening again. Dad worked it out. Now I'm startin' to. Doesn't matter what we do.

DAISY: What *we* do?

NOAH: It won't change anything.

DAISY: You're *doing* fucking nothing. There's a difference between not going above and beyond, and literally doing nothing. You don't even show up at dinner. We have to try to be normal if we want things to go back to normal.

NOAH: Well you, and me, and Mum, none of us are normal, alright. And I'm starting to think that if you reckon someone's normal, it just means you don't know 'em well enough.

A car horn is heard from out front.

DAISY: That's Meg.

NOAH: I need to get dressed.

DAISY *goes to leave the room, then turns back to* NOAH.

DAISY: I found your jacket. Dad's jacket.

NOAH: …

DAISY: The one in the box you hid in your wardrobe.

NOAH: I wasn't hiding it. I was storing it. There's a difference.

DAISY: Mum was wearing it this morning when I found her. So at least she didn't chuck it out.

SCENE TWELVE

The bus stop on Daisy Moon's front lawn. Much later that day.

DAISY *sits on the bench, strumming ukulele chords.*

PARKER *enters.*

PARKER: Where were ya this morning?

Pause.

We were meant to line up for tickets, in case you forgot?

DAISY: I didn't forget.

PARKER: Why are you upset?

Long pause.

You mad at me or something?

DAISY: No.

PARKER: Well, you seem mad at me.

DAISY: Guess you're not very good at reading people then.

Pause.

PARKER: Well, next time you bail on me, it'd be nice to have a heads-up. I waited ages for you, then went into town and lined up by myself. But by the time I got to the front of the line it was way too late, because I waited freaking ages for you!

DAISY: Parker?

PARKER: What?

DAISY: Can you just—?

Isabelle Ford (left) as Daisy and Ayeesha Ash as Parker in the Q Theatre production at the Joan Sutherland Performing Arts Centre, Penrith, in 2017. (Photo: Katy Green Loughrey)

[*Holding back*] Can you please leave me alone?

PARKER: If you're mad at me about yesterday—

DAISY: I'm not mad at you.

PARKER: What does it matter if I'm friends with Noah?

DAISY: Rack off.

PARKER: We're just *friends*, what's the big deal?

DAISY: Well, that's clearly a lie.

PARKER: So I guess I can go to the party? Now we can't go to the concert.

DAISY: I guess you can.

PARKER: Then I will.

DAISY: I guess there's no point working at the tuckshop now the concert's sold out.

PARKER: No point?

DAISY: I mean, that's the whole reason I got the job in the first place. There's no *other* reason for me to work there.

PARKER: Right.

> *Pause.*

DAISY: So you can leave now.

> PARKER *stares at* DAISY. *Doesn't move.*

Seriously, Parker. This is my spot. My clubhouse. I got here first. Now rack off, will you?

> *Pause.*

PARKER: The graffiti wasn't me.

DAISY: What?

PARKER: I don't care if you're gay. If you are, then, it's okay.

DAISY: … I'm not.

PARKER: Okay.

> PARKER *takes a seat next to* DAISY.

But it's okay if you are.

DAISY: Leave me alone or I swear I will never speak to you ever again.

> PARKER *stares at* DAISY, *doesn't know what to say.*

> *After a long moment.*

PARKER: Fine.

> PARKER *leaves.*

DAISY *sits alone. She sighs. Puts her head in her hands. Spots her bangles. Glockenspiel musical scales and a UFO whirr melodically in the air.* GAGA *is present.*

GAGA: Well, that didn't go to plan.

DAISY: No shit.

GAGA: You can't force these things, Daisy. You don't need to fit in.

DAISY: Not now, Gaga.

GAGA: You wanna stand out. Way out. So far out they'll think you were from outta space.

DAISY: You know what? I don't believe in you anymore. You hear me? Get outta here!

GAGA: Out of where?

DAISY: Out of my head!

DAISY *takes off her bangles. Then takes off her crown. Then takes off all of her clothes and accessories until she's sitting in her underwear and plain cotton singlet.*

The UFO whirr stops. GAGA *is gone.*

SCENE THIRTEEN

The creek.

NOAH *sits on the rocks.* JIMMY *spots him from the overpass.*

JIMMY: You training this arvo?

NOAH: Nup.

JIMMY: You look like shit.

NOAH: Where you headed?

JIMMY: Chicken shop.

Pause.

Heard 'bout ya mum.

NOAH: Is nothing private in this town?

JIMMY: My sister was the nurse registrar on.

NOAH: …

JIMMY: I didn't tell anyone.

Pause.

I don't get suicide.

NOAH: I think I get it.

Pause.

I wouldn't do it, but I think I get it.

JIMMY: I don't get it.

NOAH: Tried burning myself on the stove once.

JIMMY: You depressed now?

NOAH: Wanted to know what it felt like.

JIMMY: Ten bucks the answer was 'hot'.

> NOAH *smiles. Not at the joke, but because* JIMMY *is familiar.*

You always been way too in ya head, mate.

> *Pause.*

Hey, you alright?

> NOAH *avoids eye contact.*

What's been going on with ya? You're not you.

NOAH: Don't know who I am without swimming.

> It's like, how am I meant to start again when I don't even know who I am?
>
> I'm just faking it because—
>
> Actually I dunno why. But I am.
>
> Everything about me is so fucking fake.

> *Long pause.*

JIMMY: I fake praying sometimes.

NOAH: What?

JIMMY: When my grandparents come for dinner. Mum makes us all fake it. Say grace at the table and everything.

NOAH: It's not the same.

JIMMY: I fake smoking at parties. Just bum puff. Ciggies taste rank.

NOAH: For real?

JIMMY: Truth. Everyone's always faking stuff.

NOAH: I fake being a gracious winner. Out loud I'm like, 'Hey, mate, great race, you were awesome out there, I was worried for a moment'. But inside I'm like, 'Eat shit, loser, I fucking beat ya'. That's full narcissist, hey?

> *Pause.*

Sorry I was completely shit to you.

JIMMY: …

NOAH: We cool?

JIMMY: You know what, Noah? You're so focussed on being a winner. It's like your whole identity is about winning. So you go lookin' for losers. Lookin' for people you can point to and say, 'Those people there, they're the losers', so you can be propped up by them. And I don't wanna be that person for you.

   Pause.

NOAH: You reckon we should do this abalone thing?

JIMMY: I reckon you're way better than someone who bails on their family. But yeah … if it were me, I'd do it.

   PARKER *enters.*

PARKER: Hey.

NOAH: Hey.

JIMMY: So you going to this party with my boy Noah or what?

PARKER: Nup.

JIMMY: Ouch. Straight-up rejection.

PARKER: Can't. Won't be here.

NOAH: Since when?

PARKER: Since this afternoon. My parents called. They got the posting in Berlin. Going back to Melbourne to say 'bye to everyone.

NOAH: Berlin? Berlin's a whole world away.

PARKER: Same world.

NOAH: Whole other side of the world.

PARKER: I'll be total Euro-trash. So that's pretty cool. Tomorrow's my last night.

NOAH: So no party?

PARKER: Can't. Catching the red-eye bus back to Melbourne.

   Pause.

NOAH: Berlin, huh?

PARKER: Yep. New house. New school. New friends.

   Pause.

   Do you miss your old school?

NOAH: I mean, the boys ratted on me so …

   Pause.

   Actually, yeah. Yeah, I really miss 'em.

SCENE FOURTEEN

Noah's bedroom. The following day.

DAISY *lies on Noah's bed, playing with his portable radio.*

She clicks the radio on, static from terrible reception crackles.

She adjusts the dial until she finds a station.

Katy Perry's 'I Kissed a Girl' plays.

DAISY: Nope!

> DAISY *tries to find another station. Static again. She keeps adjusting the dial until she finds one. Classical music plays.*

No.

> DAISY *adjusts the dial. Static again.*

VOICE ON RADIO: [*an old male with a thick Australian accent*] What I'm saying, Ray, what I'm saying here is that it would be folly to expect that women will ever dominate simply because their aptitudes and interests are different to men for biological reasons—

DAISY: Eugh! Morons!

> NOAH *enters.* DAISY *clicks the radio off.*

NOAH: Mum's getting home some time after three. Meg said they're just waiting to speak to the outpatient nurse.

DAISY: What's the time now?

NOAH: Two thirty.

DAISY: Is that what you're wearing?

NOAH: Yeah, why?

DAISY: Shouldn't we dress nice or something?

> NOAH *shrugs.*
>
> *Long pause.*

She'll never be happy, hey?

NOAH: You know, maybe she'll be better this time.

DAISY: Coz you're here.

> *They smile at each other.*

You think I have a weird face shape?

NOAH: I mean … sorta. You look a lot like Dad actually.

DAISY: This guy I kissed told me that I have a weird face shape.
NOAH: Guy you kissed?
DAISY: Yeah.
NOAH: Who?
DAISY: Not telling.
NOAH: Who?
DAISY: Johnno.
NOAH: Huh. I thought …
        For some reason I thought—
DAISY: What?
NOAH: Nothing.
DAISY: Tell.
NOAH: Some people told me you, you know, like girls.
DAISY: Oh.

> *Pause.*

> Don't know yet really. But I kissed some guys before. And a girl.

> *Pause.*

> So that's a thing.

NOAH: Yeah.
DAISY: And now you know.
NOAH: Now I know.

> *Pause.*

DAISY: I kissed Georgia at her birthday.
NOAH: Georgia Dixon?
DAISY: She said if I told anyone, she'd make sure no-one ever talked
        to me again. I didn't tell or nothing. But I stopped getting invited
        to things.
NOAH: …
DAISY: Now you go.
NOAH: I go?
DAISY: I told you a secret, now it's your go.
NOAH: I don't have any secrets.
DAISY: Noah?

> *Pause.*

> Noah. James. Moon.

NOAH: I didn't take steroids.

DAISY: What?

NOAH: I didn't take steroids. I just said I did. To take the fall for some other students.

DAISY: Why?

NOAH: It's terrible.

DAISY: Noah!

NOAH: If Mum and Dad find out …

I don't want 'em to think I was actually good enough and ruined it. I figure they'll get over it faster if they think I wasn't good enough in the first place.

DAISY: What happened then?

NOAH: My roommate in the dorms had ADHD. Which means the world moves super fast for him, so he takes meds to slow him down. But for someone like you, or someone like me, well if we took his meds they'd speed us right up.

He heard a lotta people take 'em to do well in exams. And you don't keep your scholarship if you can't average Cs. Plus with squad there's so many hours of training on top of school.

It didn't feel like cheating. It's not like copying the answers, or getting another kid to write your essay. You still gotta show up and do the work. Just gives ya energy to pull all-nighters.

One of the scholarship boys in water polo's grades were slipping. He just lost it. Kept repeating, 'I'm fucked, I'm fucked, I'm fucked …'

So I thought, 'Alright, I'll tell him 'bout the meds'. I'm not selfish. I didn't want to keep the secret for myself. So I let him in on it, and explained about Alex and ADHD meds, and how it's like taking speed.

And he just said, 'How much do I owe ya?'

Hadn't even occurred to me to sell it. I was just trying to help a mate out.

So I said, 'Nah, don't worry about it'.

And he said, 'Cool. I'll fix you up next time'.

And next time became the next exam, and the exam after that, and soon the entire swim team's in on it.

Had it timed perfectly with time trials. They randomly test your piss so you gotta be careful. But it's easy coz trials were always the week before exams. So you compete clean. Take Ritalin to study. Sit the exam. Rinse and repeat.

And I dunno, we started getting cocky.

Josh had the idea that we could make money if we sold it to other students.

So we start selling it. Find kids who want to cash in on their diagnosis. Recruit some other kids who can fake it to get a prescription.

And it wasn't just me. It was Josh's idea to sell it, and the guys were all getting a cut.

Anyway. At Regionals a kid gets done for steroids. No-one had any idea. It's all over the newspapers coz he was tiny, like thirteen, it was totally messed up.

So the school's freaking out because they'll lose funding if it's linked to their coaches. So all of a sudden there's mandatory drug tests for every single athlete on campus.

I'm in R.E. when it's announced over the loudspeaker. Takes us totally by surprise. And the boys start freaking out like, 'What the fuck are we gonna do?! We're fucked. We're gonna go to jail.' Which is mental because we definitely won't, but they're idiots and they're freaking out. Harry's saying we need to flat-out refuse to take the test. Matt says something about getting other kids to piss in a cup for us.

And I'm like, 'Relax, we just need to come clean to Coach. We didn't cheat at the swimming. That's what we say straight out. We didn't cheat at the swimming.'

But the boys went real weird. I could tell 'coming clean' wasn't how they do things. Josh tells me I need to keep my mouth shut.

And so I did. I take the test. And I keep my mouth shut.

Two days later I'm called into the principal's office. And all my teammates are standing outside in the hallway. Matt, Josh, Conrad, and Harry. With their parents, all in suits, obviously, because their jobs are fancy.

I look around for Dad coz I wanna explain to him before we have to go in. But I can't see Dad with the boys so I assume he's in the office.

And I'm like, okay, keep it cool, explain you didn't cheat at swimming. That's all you gotta say.

And I go inside.
But it's just the principal and Josh's dad.

I'm asked to take a seat, and then the principal is telling me that four other students have come forward with a signed statement saying that I was selling drugs to the entire Year Eleven cohort.

And I tell him, 'It's bullshit, it was Josh's idea, just ask him'.

And Josh's dad is telling me to be careful about what I say, because it'll be used against me.

'What do you mean used against me?'
And the principal says, 'These are criminal charges, Noah. Fraud. Sale of controlled substances. Drug trafficking.'
'Where's my dad, I wanna talk to my dad!'
'We called him, Noah, but he didn't call us back. So we're settling this inside the school to avoid any further embarrassment.'

And I think, sweet. Get outta jail free card.

'So unfortunately, Noah, you're going to have to say you tested positive to steroids.'
'No way. I didn't even take 'em. Ask the boys, get them in here, get them to explain.'

And Josh's Dad leans over, real menacing, and says real quiet, 'If you speak to any of the them, say anything to them, we'll get the police involved'.

And I realise that those people outside the office, the ones in suits, they're lawyers.
They've pinned it on me. All of it.
They're untouchable.
To them I'm just some country kid whose dad didn't show, and the only thing they'll give me is a shit deal to save their own asses.
I wanna say, get stuffed, I didn't take 'em!
But I'm scared of what'll happen, so …
I take the deal.
Say I took steroids.

Everything.
Fucking gone.
Like that.

One shitty choice starts to fester and grow and becomes big enough to catch you. Karma, or life, or whatever, just fucking catches you, doesn't it?

S'not fair though.

It's like, there's people in this world that karma's always gonna catch up to 'em. Coz they don't have the money to run fast enough. And then there's other people who ... doesn't matter what they do. Doesn't matter what shit they pull. They get second, third, fourth, fifth chances.

They're untouchable.

Pause.

DAISY: Thanks for telling me.

Pause.

How come we can swim? Like, why can human beings even swim at all?

NOAH: No idea.

DAISY: If you had to guess.

NOAH: Maybe we were on land, but at some point for some reason we had ta learn to swim? To survive or find food, so we figured it out. And I guess our bodies would have to adapt to it.

DAISY: Right.

Pause.

But why?

NOAH: Why what?

DAISY: Why would our bodies have to adapt?

NOAH: Because we had to, to survive.

DAISY: Why?

NOAH: So that we wouldn't die.

Long pause.

It's like something in us, biologically, something within our biology wants us to keep going.

DAISY: Since the very beginning, hey?

NOAH: Yeah. Since the very beginning, we had some impulse to keep moving forward.

DAISY: Like a bass note.

Pause.

NOAH: Did Parker tell you she's leaving?

DAISY: At the end of summer? Yeah, she's just here with her gran for a bit.

NOAH: Nah, she's leaving like, right now. Packing for Melbourne.

DAISY: No way, she'd tell me.

NOAH: Her parents got the posting in Berlin. Said tonight's her last night.

DAISY: If she was leaving then she'd say goodbye.

NOAH *shrugs.*

Wouldn't she?

NOAH: Maybe not.

DAISY: … Whatever.

DAISY *clicks the radio on. The last few seconds of 'Poker Face' by Lady Gaga plays. The song finishes.*

VOICE ON RADIO: That was Lady Gaga's 'Poker Face'. She's touring Australia right now. And listeners, stay right there for your chance to win tickets to her Sydney show.

DAISY: What?!

VOICE ON RADIO: That's right. One lucky caller will have the chance to see Lady Gaga tonight at her Sydney concert at the Entertainment Centre. The concert sold out in ninety minutes last week, but this is your chance, right now, to win yourself a ticket.

DAISY: It'd never be me.

NOAH: Call anyway?

DAISY: I can't get to Sydney.

NOAH: I'll drive you. Take Meg's car. We can leave now.

VOICE ON RADIO: The number to call is 1800 GAGA. With the answer to this question: When is Lady Gaga's birthday?

DAISY: March twenty-eight!

DAISY *dials the number on her phone, brings the phone to her ear.*

VOICE ON RADIO: The number to call is 1800 GAGA.

DAISY: March twenty-seven. March twenty-eight. Same as Parker's.

Pause.

DAISY *hangs up the phone.*

I gotta say goodbye to Parker.

SCENE FIFTEEN

The bus stop on Daisy Moon's front lawn.

DAISY: Thanks for coming.

PARKER: How could I resist this text message: 'Parker. Full stop. Get your butt to the bus stop asap. PS. That's short for as soon as possible.'

DAISY: Noah told me about Berlin.

PARKER: Sucks, hey.

DAISY: You all packed up?

PARKER: Mostly.

PARKER *takes a seat next to* DAISY.

DAISY: I don't want you to leave.

PARKER: It's not coz I don't care.

DAISY: Still don't want you to.

Pause.

I guess I'm just really fucking lonely.

PARKER *leans in to kiss* DAISY.

DAISY *pulls back.*

PARKER: What?

DAISY: What did you—?

PARKER: Nothing.

DAISY: I thought.

PARKER: Thought what?

DAISY: Nothing.

PARKER: Say it.

DAISY: I thought you were—

PARKER *kisses* DAISY. *It lasts for a short moment.*

Pause.

PARKER: You don't have to say anything.
DAISY: Why'd you do that?
PARKER: Dunno.
DAISY: You do.

Pause.

PARKER: You can't stop people leaving, Daisy.

Pause.

You wanna watch Lady Gaga on tele?
DAISY: Let's go to the party. You got time?
PARKER: I got an hour.
DAISY: Then let's go to the party.

SCENE SIXTEEN

The front porch of the house party.

NOAH *sits alone on the porch. Loud music pumps from inside the house.*

DAISY *and* PARKER *arrive.*

DAISY: I love this song.
NOAH: Thought you weren't coming?
PARKER: I've got time for one dance. [*To* DAISY] Want to go inside?
DAISY: You coming, Noah?
NOAH: I like it out here.
DAISY: Sitting on the doorstep like some sorry ass alley cat?
NOAH: I like cats.
DAISY: Like some dingy old gutter puss.
NOAH: There's people from school inside.
DAISY: Scared of few drunk teenagers? What's the worst that could happen?
NOAH: Famous last words.
DAISY: Let's go in.
NOAH: I don't even like those people inside, but I still want them to like me. How two-faced is that?
DAISY: Doesn't matter if they don't like you, doesn't mean you can't exist. Why shouldn't we go in? They're just people. And it's just a party. Why shouldn't we go too? Just be yourself.

NOAH: I don't think I like myself very much.

DAISY *and* PARKER *take a seat either side of* NOAH.

Hey, what do you do when you don't feel good enough?
DAISY: You know what you do, Noah? You do Gaga.

The song from inside the house switches to 'Marry the Night' by Lady Gaga.

Most people think 'Marry the Night' is about party culture. Like, living for the night. But it's actually way deeper than that. It's about embracing the darkness inside of you. Embracing what you hide from people. You can run away from the parts of yourself that scare you, or you can accept them.

DAISY *starts dancing and singing the lyrics.*

Dance with me, Noah. Let the music fill you up and take you to another dimension within yourself.
NOAH: Absolutely not.

DAISY *takes* NOAH *by the hand.* NOAH *resists her at first, but eventually he yields.*

The siblings dance for a moment before PARKER *joins them.*

The three dance together.

It doesn't suit the music but they make it work. They laugh and enjoy the movements. None of them look cool. But they don't look embarrassed either.

THE END